Newcastle from New Chatham, Gateshead. *T. Allom, 1832*

Newcastle Castle

Newcastle was a bridge head and owed its initial foundation to its position on the River Tyne. Here the Romans built a bridge and established a fort (probably on the site of Collingwood Street) to defend it. However its name is derived from the Norman Castle built here over 800 years ago.

In 1080 Robert Curthose, the eldest son of William the Conqueror, made an expedition into Scotland and on his return "laid the foundation of a castle whereby the town of Newcastle did afterwards both take her beginning and her name" (Speed). The chosen site was very strong. On three sides it was defended by precipitous banks reaching to the Lort Burn and the Tyne. On the west only was the ground comparatively level and here a ditch was built.

Of this early Norman castle nothing remains. It was a normal motte and bailey fortress built of earth and wood. Such a castle was not strong enough to resist a powerful opponent and in 1095 it was captured during the revolt of the Norman barons and retaken later by William Rufus.

This original earthen castle was replaced by a stone fortress in the reign of Henry II. In 1155 Henry took over the former royal castles and ordered the destruction of the unlicensed castles which had been built during the civil wars of the previous reign. Three years later the earldom of Northumberland reverted to the crown and as a basis for military operations against the Scots, the present keep was begun in 1172 and was completed in 1177. The architect or military engineer was one Maurice who a few years later designed the tower at Dover. **The keep** is a typical example of transitional architecture. It is roughly square, measuring 18.9 x 17.1m [62 x 56 feet], excluding the fore building. Three corners are covered by square projections and the fourth is a polygonal tower. The interior comprises three floors each of which consists of a principal apartment with subsidiary apartments and stairs in the thick walls. The walls are carried above the roof for defence but the battlements are all restoration. From the basement floor to the top of the modern flat roof the height is 24.7m [81ft]. The walls are in places 5.5m [18ft] in thickness resting on a massive plinth of nine chamfered courses. The stone is sandstone.

Castle, Newcastle *T. Allom, 1832*

The **entrance** to the keep is by an external staircase which was protected by three towers. The lower tower is now gone. Ascending 23 steps we come to the gate tower. A little beyond on either side of the stair is a small lamp niche with dished sill for oil. Ascending another 14 steps we come to the landing and the third tower which was used as a guardroom. The interior is entirely modern.

A short flight of steps leads to the great doorway of the keep. The original was destroyed in the great explosion at Gateshead in 1854 but the restoration is a faithful reproduction. Through a barrel-vaulted passage we enter the Great Hall.

The **Great Hall** measures 9.1 x 7.3m [30 x 24ft] and the ceiling, built in 1813, is arched with its crown more than 12.2m [40ft] from the floor. The original roof was lower and did not include the upper windows. To the south in the thickness of the wall is a room 6.7 x 2.4m [22 x 8ft] in size, called the King's Chamber. It is well lit by three good windows and contains an original fireplace with an arched head. The north wall is inscribed with many names probably those of prisoners detained here at various times. In the north-east turret is a vaulted chamber known as the well-room. The well is 30.2m [99ft] deep and the depth of water is 15.2m [50ft]. On either side of the well are basins in recesses with pipe holes whereby water was transmitted to the lower parts of the castle.

Descending by the mural stair we enter the first floor apartment. It measures 8.2 x 6.7m [27 x 22ft] and is lighted by four windows. The pier in the middle and the arches which rest on it are modern.
In the north wall is a large barrel-vaulted apartment usually called the Queen's Chamber which contains an original fireplace.

The main compartment in the basement is the **Garrison Room**. It is remarkable for its fine vault which is supported by a circular central pier with an octagonal scalloped capital from which radiate eight chamfered ribs dividing the ceiling into eight cells.

The **Chapel** is an interesting portion of the castle and occupies the whole of the basement below the forebuilding. "Although very ornate, the work is not an example of thoughtful construction. It is very irregular in design and execution. The adjacent parts are clumsily brought together and rude in workmanship as compared with Maurice the architect's work at Dover" (W.H.Knowles). The external walls of the chapel are very thin, only 84cm [2.75ft], but originally there was no direct communication between it and the interior of the tower. It consists of a chancel with a nave or ante-chapel at right angles.

After the keep was built the wooden palisade surrounding the original bailey was replaced by a stone curtain wall and in this greatly strengthened courtyard detached residential buildings arose comprising a hall, chamber, kitchen and stables. They were built against the east curtain wall which was the most difficult to attack. Nothing remains of these buildings.

In 1247 the **Black Gate** was added at a cost of over £500. Later, in 1358, a barbican, of which no trace remains, was added in front of the gate. The height of the Black Gate today is 19.2m [63ft] but since the upper storeys have been extensively altered we cannot determine the original height.

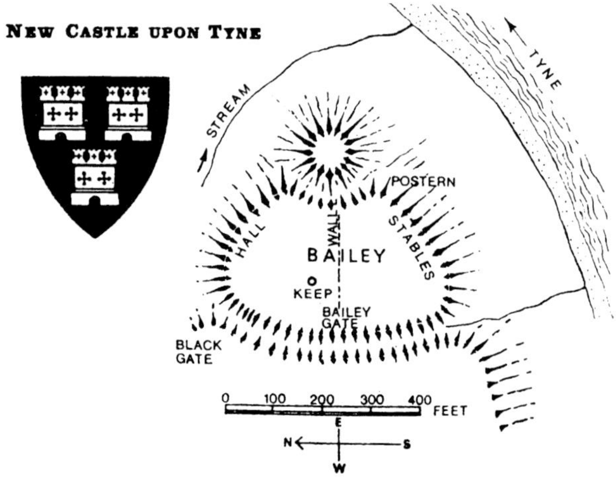

The entrance is within a square projection carried to the roof with buttresses on either side containing trefoil headed niches. The mullioned windows are Jacobean. The entrance passage is 10.4m [34ft] long with a pointed barrel vault. It was closed by a drawbridge. One-and-a-half metres [5ft] within was the portcullis

The Blackgate *W. Brook, 1896*

whose groove can be seen and 3.4m [11ft] further was the gate. After passing two recesses on either side we come to the entrance to the guard-chambers.

How the first floor was entered is uncertain since the present staircase is modern. The second and third floors with their mullioned windows are the work of those who followed Alexander Stevenson to whom the building was leased in 1618.

After passing through the Black Gate there is an open court in which is situated the Heron Pit which is an underground prison named after William Heron of Ford, sheriff of Northumberland and governor of the castle from 1247 to 1257.

After the building of the town walls about 1280 and the subsequent building of the great gates the military importance of the castle declined and it was allowed to fall into decay. In 1334 Roger Mauduyt, then Sheriff of Northumberland reported that "The castle of New Castle on Tyne is so decayed and so left to neglect that there is not in all the castle a single house where one can have shelter, nor any gate which can be closed".

In 1400 Newcastle became an independent county but the castle remained as part of Northumberland. By this time the keep became the county gaol and the great hall in the bailey was the assize court. They were known respectively as the High Castle and the Moot Hall. Since the Newcastle authorities had no jurisdiction in the area of the castle they had great difficulty in arresting criminals who took refuge there. It was not until 1589 that a charter of Queen Elizabeth solved this problem.

The castle was last used for warlike purposes during the Civil War, in the siege of 1644. Thereafter it had a number of tenants who allowed the various buildings to fall into decay. The chapel in the courtyard had become an inn called the Three Bulls' Heads and its cellar was the more famous chapel inside the castle. In 1787 John Howard the famous prison reformer visited Newcastle. He tells us that "during the assizes at Newcastle, the county prisoners are, men and women, confined together seven or eight nights, in a dirty damp dungeon, six steps in the old castle, which, having no roof, in wet season the water is some inches deep. The felons are chained to rings in the wall". On the assize Sunday the prisoners were exhibited to the public, "and the vulgar and curious paid sixpence each for admission". In 1810 the Corporation of Newcastle purchased the keep and started to restore it adding the castellated battlements. In recent times the Black Gate and the keep have been extensively repaired.

Next to the castle stands Newcastle Cathedral.

Newcastle Cathedral

The Cathedral Church of St Nicholas belongs almost entirely to the 14th and 15th centuries. Its outstanding feature is the famous lantern tower which features prominently in most views of old Newcastle.

The church is first mentioned in 1122 although probably built some years earlier. Twice almost destroyed

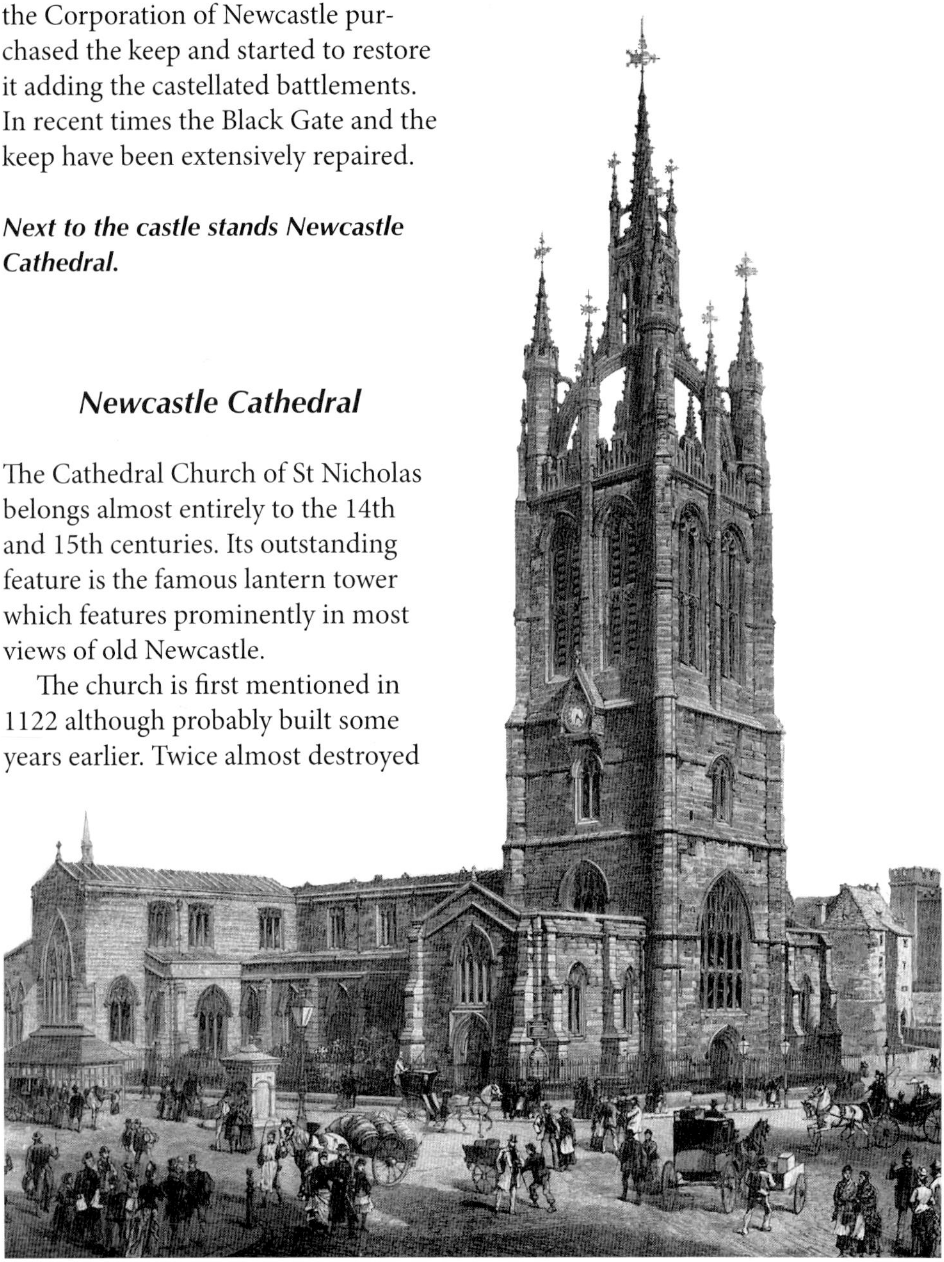

by fire in the 13th century the work of reconstruction was started in the 14th century and completed in 1448 with the addition of the beautiful lantern. The interior was richly endowed with monuments, altars and stained glass, most of which was swept away in the Reformation. Only an almost unique eagle lectern, a font with carved oak cover and some fragments of glass have survived from the rich interior.

In 1730 a new library and vestry were added to the church and from 1783 extensive alterations and repairs were carried out, principally under the direction of the famous architect John Dobson. The tower was in such a bad state that it had to be supported on the south side by enormous buttresses. When in 1882 the See of Newcastle was founded and St Nicholas became the Cathedral Church many additions were made including a reredos, a Bishop's throne, a pulpit and choir stalls.

The visitor enters the church by the tower with its famous lantern, a type called the Scottish Crown, an example of which can he seen at St Giles in Edinburgh. The base of the tower was used as a baptistery the fine lierne vaulting of which is inscribed with the name of Robert Rodes the donor. Above the baptistery are the ringing chamber and the belfry which contains 17 bells the three earliest dating from about 1400. The porches or transepts on either side of the tower contain a number of interesting monuments. The lofty but narrow nave was completed in 1359 and is lighted by a clerestory with triple lancets. The aisles are very wide

with octagonal pillars. Between the nave and the chancel is the crossing with two pointed arches. The fine rood screen which separates the nave from the chancel was added in 1882. The 14th century choir has a magnificent heraldic roof and an imposing reredos of Uttoxceter alabaster.

After inspecting the choir the visitor can then look at the transepts and the numerous chapels with monuments to many worthies of our city, the two most interesting being the memorial to the Maddison family (Henry Maddison was Mayor in 1623 and 1624) on the west wall of the south transept and the monument to William Hall, who died in 1634, in St George's Chapel. He also was a Mayor of Newcastle. Both these monuments are the work of Nicholas Stone, master mason to James I and Charles I.

When leaving the church the visitor should see the churchyard. In the south-east corner is a monument to the famous engraver Thomas Bewick whose workshop once stood here.

From the cathedral we go down the Side, a narrow and steep street, once the most picturesque in the town, but no old buildings are left on this historic thoroughfare.

Newcastle from The Side *T. Allom, 1832*

Sand Hill, Newcastle *T. Allom, 1832*

Sandhill

The Side leads us to the **Sandhill** which occupies an important place in the history of Newcastle. It was the centre of the medieval city and the group of large and handsome old timbered houses still standing remind us of this great past.

The Guildhall, with its centuries of historic associations, still remains as a memorial to the early civic and social history of Newcastle. The first Exchange or Town Hall was built early in the 15th century. But in 1655 it was pulled down and replaced by a handsome Guildhall erected in the Italian manner by Robert Trollop. According to the articles of agreement, in the archives of the town, he agreed to build it for £2.000, but Bourne says it cost upwards of £10,000. The original building was of great beauty and "withal very sumptuous". It has undergone numerous external and internal alterations in 1794 and 1809. The whole front was encased in freestone, the old steeple and staircase taken down, and the front rebuilt.

The interior is of great beauty. The most important room is the Merchants' Court. With its fine panelled walls, its magnificently decorated ceiling and its beautifully carved overmantel it stands as a monument to a wealthy and important city.

The Guildhall and Fish Market *old print*

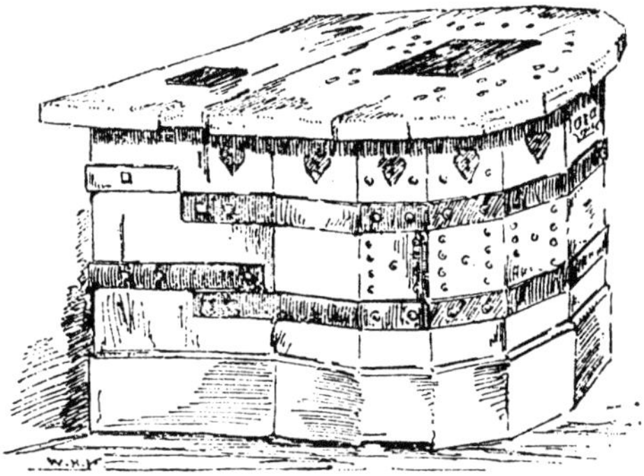

The Town Hutch in the Guildhall was used for storing the corporation money. In 1740 the poor townsfolk rioted on account of the high price of food and broke into the Guildhall rifling the Town Hutch.

Of the fine houses still remaining, **Surtees and Milbank House**, which are now really one, are perhaps the best known. Surtees House is recorded as being owned by Robert Rhodes in 1465, though it is not likely that he lived here. He was a lawyer and man of wealth. To him we owe the steeple of St Nicholas. He died in 1474 leaving no children. We first hear of the house to the west of Surtees House as being owned by the chaplain of the chantry of St John the Baptist and St John the Evangelist in St Nicholas Church, which is reputed to have been re-founded by Robert Rhodes in 1461. It seems likely that, as today, the two houses were thus originally under the same ownership.

The Merchant's Court, Guildhall

Surtees House to many people is known only because it recalls the run-away marriage of Bessie Surtees. During the last quarter of the eighteenth century Surtees House was occupied by Aubone Surtees, a banker and prominent citizen of Newcastle. Of his eight children the eldest daughter, Elizabeth, was considered a great beauty. "Before she had attained the age of eighteen", a relative writes, "her hand was sought for by the flower of the surrounding squirearchy". At the same time however there lived close by in Love Lane a coal-fitter, called William Scott. One of his three sons, John, fell in love with Bessie Surtees and the two lovers met in secret. On the night of 18th November, 1772 they eloped and crossed the Border where they were married according to Scottish law at Blackshields. John Scott, many years later, became Lord Eldon and Chancellor of England.

Surtees House and Milbank House are now joined together and the name Surtees House usually covers both. There are many fine rooms inside. The large room on the first floor is the finest in the house. The window used by Bessie Surtees

is marked with a blue pane. The room is panelled in oak, the beautifully figured oak panels being relieved at intervals by ribbed pillars, which are terminated with carved cherubs' heads.

The large open fireplace is dated 1657 and is surmounted by an elaborately and tastefully carved overmantel. The centre panel of the mantel is carved with the twin arcade motif popular in Newcastle and the panels on either side have a geometric design. The panels are flanked by Ionic pillars and the whole is carried on pillars of the same type from the floor.

In the cornice above the pillars are carved four shields bearing arms. The first shield bears the arms of Newcastle upon Tyne, the second those of the Cock family, the third those of Davison, and the fourth those of the Merchant Adventurers' Company. At the base of the four pillars in the same order are the following word, ciphers, and date: ANNO AC TD 1657. T.D. are the initials of Thomas Davison who was mayor of Newcastle in 1669 and governor of the Merchants' Company in 1670, A.C. are those of his wife Ann Cock.

The stuccoed ceiling of the room is a reproduction of the ceiling in Cosin's House which was of the same date and once stood near the corner of the Sandhill on the site now occupied by the piers of Tyne Bridge. At the back of the fireplace in this and the adjoining room are cast iron plates with the royal arms. They were placed there in order to retain and throw out the heat.

Of the seven old houses standing in Sandhill today five are now in one unit called the **Red House**. These five houses all probably date back to the sixteenth century. Starting from the east the first house is the brick fronted building which was the original Red House. As the advert which we reproduce shows it was occupied in 1863 by the Wholesale Tea Warehouse of Probert and Co. Two fires within recent years have destroyed many of the original oak beams but the

opposite: Surtees House by T.M. Richardson. Lithograph 1844

building has been restored in good taste. At the rear of the main room is the cellar bar with walls of stone and rounded roof of bricks. This part of the house is probably the oldest fragment of building surviving on the Sandhill today.

To the west of the original Red House are two timber framed houses whose facades date from the 17th century. There have been considerable alterations to their interiors. The finest room is now the large main dining room formed from at least two rooms of the original buildings. It has two interesting stone fireplaces and a magnificent length of windows. The fourth house from the east is brick fronted.

Next to it, and adjoining Bessie Surtees House is another timber framed house, for many years occupied by a shipping firm. The main room on the second floor is the gem of the Red House. It is beautifully panelled in oak, with a magnificently carved fireplace overmantel of the same material. The overmantel is inscribed with the words ANNO W.R. 1658. The back and sides of the fireplace are lined with over one hundred fine old Dutch tiles with Chinese designs, each tile having a different picture. They are probably over three hundred years old and extremely rare. The windows are double and those inside were probably constructed in the 19th century. They have three interesting designs in coloured glass. The first design shows the town arms, the second is that of the shipping company who had offices here, the third depicts the Guildhall which stands opposite across the road. The richly ornamented ceiling is made of painted pewter.

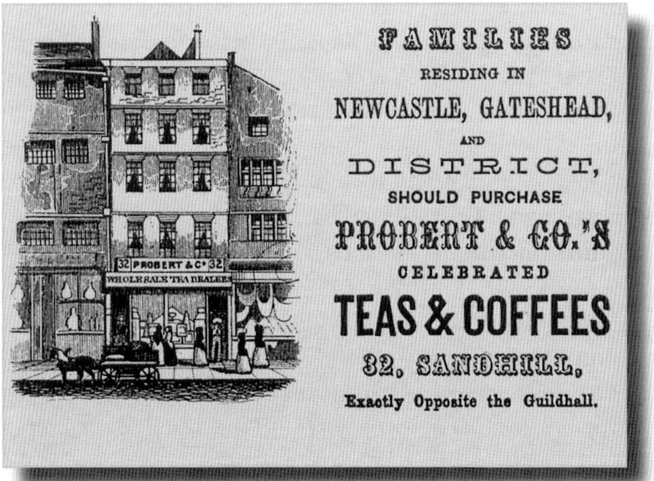

Advert of 1863 showing the original Red House.

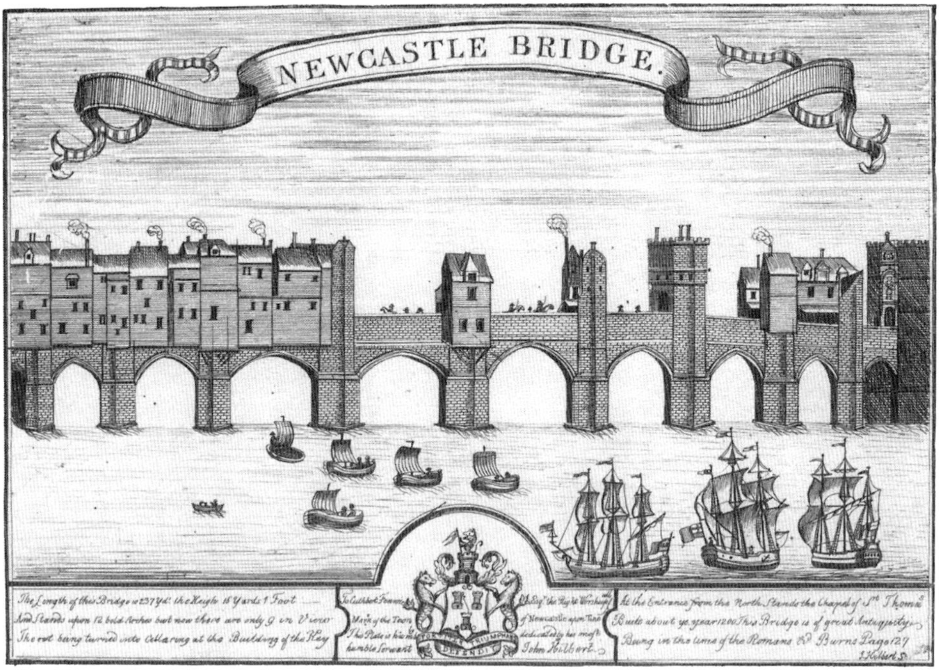

The old medieval bridge

Quayside

From the Sandhill the Tyne is crossed by the Swing Bridge . This is on the site of the Roman bridge called Pons Aelii built by the Emperor Hadrian about 120AD. It seems to have continued in use until 1248. It was replaced by the famous medieval bridge which had shops built on it like London Bridge. This was swept away in the Great Tyne Flood of 1771. A new bridge was built ten years later. However this stone bridge was so low that only small boats could pass up the river. With the development of the river and the growing trade of Newcastle the bridge became an obstruction which prevented large boats passing up the river, therefore it was removed and replaced by the present **Swing Bridge** between 1866 and 1876. The Swing Bridge was one of the first large opening bridges in the world. It was built by the Tyne Commission with Sir W.G. Armstrong and Co. as contractor.

It is 171m [560ft] long and 14.5m [47½ft] wide. The weight of the swinging portion of the bridge, 85.6m [281ft] long, is about 1,500 tons, and about 900 tons of this weight floats on a centre water press 1.57m [62 ins] in diameter with a hydraulic pressure on this press of 700 lbs per square inch. The machinery for turning the bridge is on the centre pier and is in duplicate. The bridge is turned by

The High Level Bridge and Swing Bridge looking towards Newcastle. *Etching, c. 1890*

an hydraulic engine working at 700 lbs. per square inch, the hydraulic power being generated by steam power, and only about one ton of coal per week is required for working the bridge . The cost of the Swing Bridge was £240,000.

The coming of the railway raised the question of a high level bridge across the river. One of the greatest engineers of the day, Robert Stephenson, was engaged to carry out the project. Work was started in 1846 and completed in 1849. Along with Stephenson, an engineer called Thomas Eliot Harrison worked on the scheme.

The **High Level Bridge** consists of six cast iron arches of 38m [125ft] each supported on piers of masonry. In order to reduce the weight as much as possible the lofty stone piers were built hollow from a point a little above high water mark. The length of the viaduct is 408m [1,337ft] and the height from high water to the carriageway is 25.9m [85ft]. Almost 5,000 tons of cast and wrought iron were supplied by Hawks, Crawshaw and Company of Gateshead and Losh, Wilson and Bell of Walker. The total cost of the bridge was nearly half a million pounds and as an outstanding example of engineering skill it is one of the wonders of the Railway Age.

From the Sandhill we can walk along the Quayside, once the commercial and trading centre of the town.

Sir William Brenton (1635) described the Quayside as "the finest quay in England I have met withal". Bourne the famous Newcastle historian wrote in 1736: "This street is chiefly inhabited by such as have their living by Shipping, such as Merchants, Hostmen, Brewers etc. As it is the great Place of Resort for the business of the Coal-trade (the grand Support of this Town and Country, and many other Places also) and likewise for many other Things; it is not much to be wondered at, if in going along it, you see almost nothing but a whole Street of Sign-posts of Taverns, Ale-houses, Coffee-houses etc."

Riverside Newcastle was divided into two sections by the bridge. The part below was the Quay built only on the north side. But above the Quay only small vessels could pass so here the roadway was built up on both sides and was called **The Close**.

Bourne (1736) wrote about this old Street: "It was formerly that Part of the Town where the principal Inhabitants liv'd . . . And indeed however the Street itself may be, however mean the Fronts of the Houses are, within they speak Magnificense and Grandeur, the Rooms being very large and stately, and for the most part adorn'd with cuirious Carving . . . Of late years these Houses have been forsaken, and their wealthier Inhabitants have chosen the higher Parts of the Town."

The only survivor of these houses is situated almost below the piers of the High Level Bridge. Known as **The Cooperage** it is one of the oldest houses in Newcastle. Here for many years the family of Arthur carried on the old trade of the cooper.

The Cooperage

Trinity House chapel and hospital, 1827

One of the finest buildings to be seen on the Quayside today is the Custom House. It was built in 1765. But further along we come to Broad Chare. In this street leading off from the Quayside is one of the treasures of Newcastle, **Trinity House**. It is perhaps the most interesting building in the city. Both inside and out is has never been mauled by planners and the visitor cannot but be enthralled by the countless things of interest and beauty to be seen.

Trinity House is the home of the ancient guild of Masters and Mariners and played an important part in developing the trade of the Tyne. In 1492 Ralph Hebborn of Heburn granted the site to The Guild of Fraternity of the Blessed Trinity of Newcastle-upon-Tyne and in 1505 "a hall, chapel, and lodgings for the brethren" were ordered to be erected. As the year passed the brethren were granted more extensive privileges and duties. In 1536 Henry VIII granted a new charter and a common seal and licensed them to "build and embattle two towers, one at the entrance of the haven of Tyne, the other on the hill adjoining, in each of which a light was to be maintained every night, for the support of which they were empowered to receive 4d. for every foreign ship and 2d. for every English vessel entering the Port of Tyne". These were the High and Low Lights at North Shields. Trinity House of course is still in operation. The building is not a museum. Most of the old city guilds have ceased to exist except for social purposes but the brethren of Trinity House continue with their work today.

The entrance hall is a room with an atmosphere and prepares one for the other magnificent rooms to be seen. It was rebuilt in 1800 and measures roughly 6.1 x 5.5m [20 x 18ft], housing a most varied collection of exhibits collected by the brethren.

From its beginning Trinity House was a religious institution. The interior fittings of the present chapel were erected in 1634. Repairs to the walls were carried out in 1651 and 1794. To the last rebuilding belong the windows in the south and east sides. The Banqueting Hall was built in 1721. It is a spacious and beautiful room panelled in mahogany with many fine pictures on the walls and a century old linoleum on the floor. The Board Room is also large with many old prints but is dominated by the beautiful painting by Peter Paul Rubens (1577-1640) called The Four Continents.

Returning to the Quayside and passing the Crown Court then bearing left along Milk Market we proceed to the Keelmen's Hospital.

The keelmen are first recorded as a fraternity in 1539. In 1697 they established a charitable fund with which they erected the **Keelmen's Hospital** in 1701. It is a fine square brick building two storeys high, "done in the form of colleges and monasteries having its low walk around in imitation of cloisters". The Bishops of Ely remarked "that he had heard of and seen many hospitals, the works of rich men, but that was the first he ever saw or heard of which had been built by the poor".

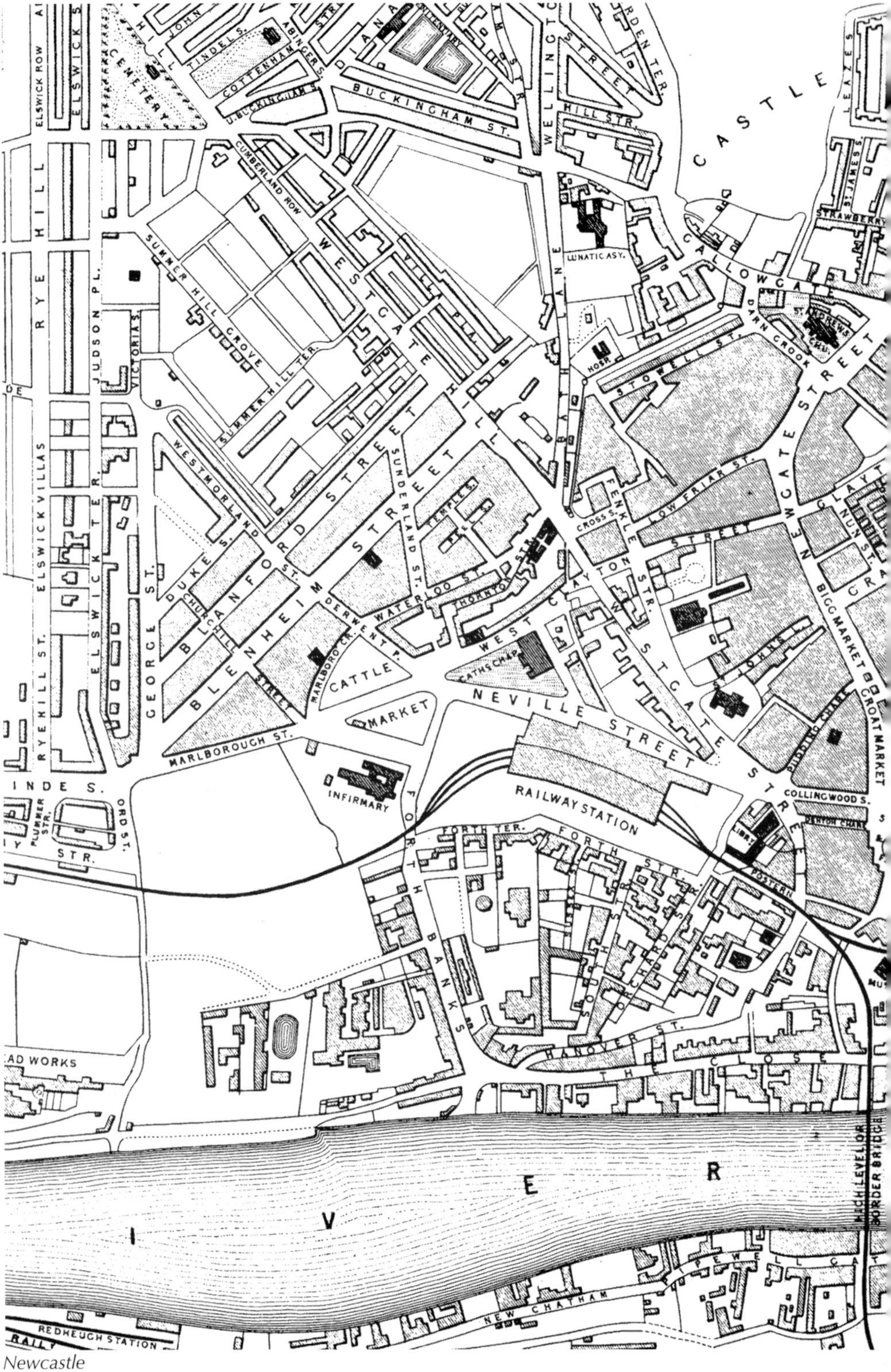
ELSWICK ROW
JOHN
TINDEL S.
ABINGER S.
CEMETERY
U. BUCKINGHAM S.
BUCKINGHAM ST.
STREET
HILL STR.
CASTLE
LEAZES
CUMBERLAND ROW
RYE HILL
SUMMER HILL GROVE
JUDSON PL.
VICTORIA S.
WESTGATE
VILL PLA.
LUNATIC ASY.
GALLOWGATE
ST. JAMES S.
STRAWBERRY
ST. ANDREWS CHU.
DARN CROOK
STOWELL ST.
HOSP.
BATH LANE
SUMMERHILL TER.
WESTMORLAND
SUNDERLAND ST.
NEWGATE STREET
LOW FRIAR ST.
FENKLE STR.
CROSS S.
NUN ST.
ELSWICK VILLAS
ELSWICK TER.
GEORGE ST.
DUKE S.
BLANFORD ST.
BLENHEIM STREET
DERWENT P.
WATERLOO ST.
WEST CLAYTON STR.
WESTGATE
BIGG MARKET
ST. JOHNS
MARLBORO CR.
CATTLE MARKET
CATHS CHAP.
NEVILLE STREET
RYEKILL ST.
CROAT MARKET
MARLBOROUGH ST.
INFIRMARY
RAILWAY STATION
COLLINGWOOD S.
PUDDING CHARE
INDE S.
PLUMBER STR.
ORD ST.
STR.
FORTH TER.
FORTH STR.
POSTERN
FORTH BANKS
HANOVER ST.
THE CLOSE
I V E R
HIGH LEVEL BR.
BORDER BRIDGE
NEW CHATHAM
REDHEUGH STATION

Newcastle

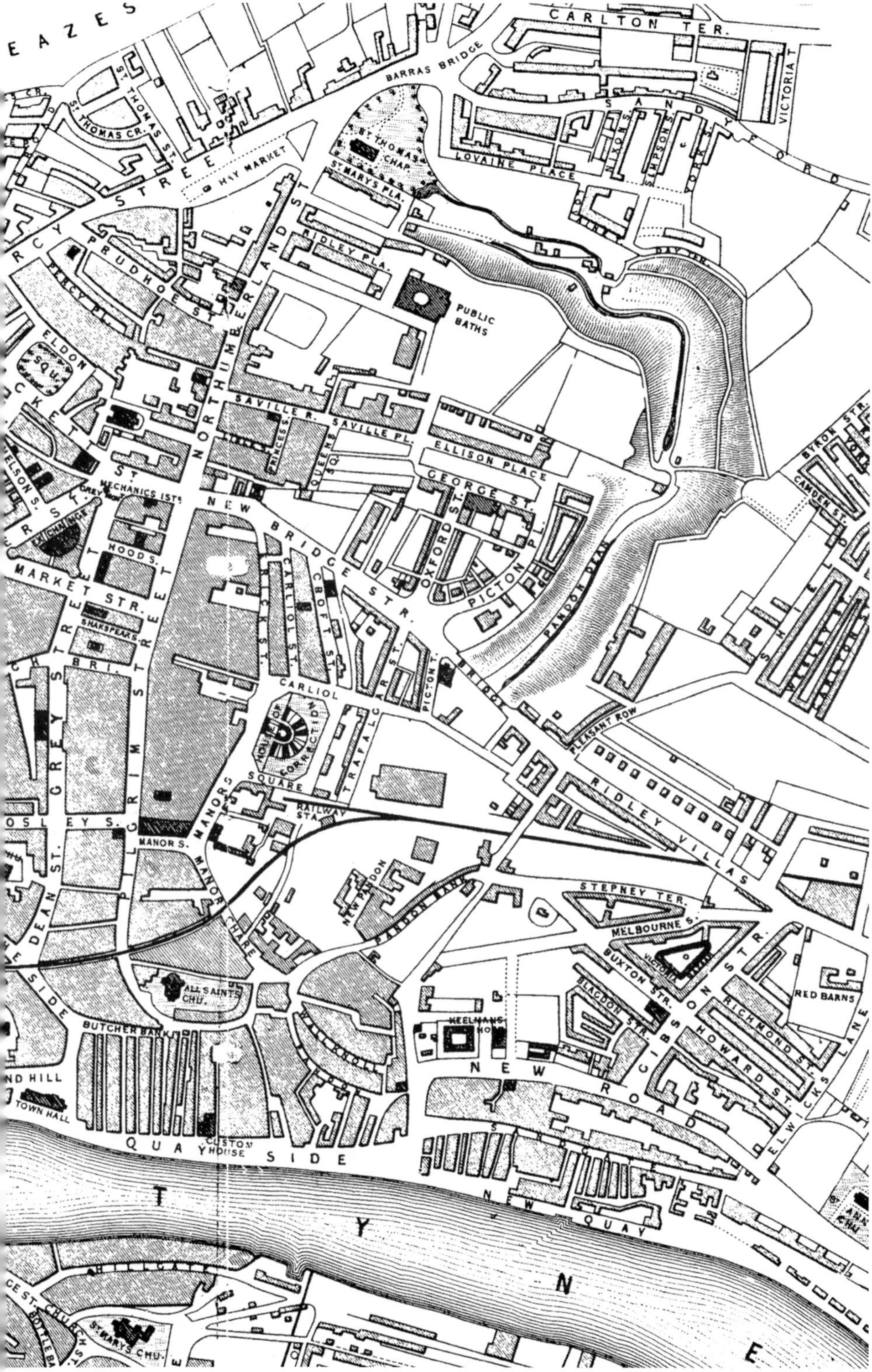

Newcastle, c.1860

J. Rankin, 1860

For many years after its foundation there was a struggle between the keelmen and the hostmen (coalowners) for control of the hospital. Although it was built and financed by the keelmen it was a struggle, in the political situation of the eighteenth century, for a working class organisation to run its own affairs without surveillance from above.

In 1730 the Keelmen formed a benefit society, and in 1788 an Act of Parliament was passed for the better regulation of this society, entitled *An Act for establishing a permanent fund for the relief and support of skippers and keelmen employed on the River Tyne, who by sickness or other accidental misfortune or by old age shall not be able to maintain themselves and families, and for the relief of widows and children of such skippers and keelmen.*

When the Society flourished, at their general annual meeting, or 'Head Meeting Day', the keelmen used to march through the town in procession, with bands of music, and afterwards dined together in state.

As a fraternity the keelemen's society decayed when modern methods were adopted for loading the colliers. The keels were no longer needed and eventually disappeared. The hospital still stands as a memorial to an important trade which once flourished in Old Newcastle.

A short distance along City Road is the church of St Ann, built in 1768 by William Newton to replace an older chapel which was much used by the keelmen. It is a fine classical church with a plain western tower.

From the Keelmen's Hospital and heading towards the city centre we reach the Holy Jesus Hospital an oasis amidst an overwhelming mass of modern buildings.

City Centre

The Holy Jesus Hospital, or as it is also called the Freemen's or Town's Hospital was founded and endowed by the Corporation of Newcastle in 1681 and built on a part of the Manors which belonged to the town. It was intended to support poor impotent people, freemen and their widows, or their sons and daughters that had never been married. It was endowed with a parcel of land in the Close, later the Mansion House was erected on that site, and property at Edderley in County Durham and Whittle in Northumberland. This endowment produced the inadequate sum of £80 a year.

In 1715 the Corporation purchased the manor of Walker for the sum of £12,200. In order to raise the money they petitioned Parliament for permission to sell the lands at Edderley and Whittle and in return for the use of the money to settle on the hospital a yearly rent charge of £185. However the bill was rejected by the House of Lords on the grounds that Walker had been purchased without the King's licence and that therefore, by the statue of mortmain, it was forfeited to the Crown. The Member of Parliament, Sir William Blackett, because he was a suspected Jacobite, was unable to get the decision rescinded. It wasn't till 1723 that a new member of Parliament, William Carr, won a pardon for the Corporation and the return of Walker. On his arrival back in Newcastle William Carr was welcomed by large crowds, with ringing of bells "and other demonstrations of joy".

Writing in 1736 Henry Bourne says, "You ascend to it by Stairs from the High Street, and then enter into a pleasing field, on the North-side of which is the said Hospital. It is three Storey high, and the Under-story is adorned with Piazza's, which are about 60 Yards in Length, and make a very agreeable Walk. About the Middle of the Piazza's is the Entrance into the second and third Stories, and over against this Entrance is a Fountain (very much beautified) for the Use of the Hospital."

In Bourne's day the 39 inmates received £4 per annum which was increased to £6 in 1769. Also they received at Christmas a fother (ton) of coal. In 1890 each occupant was paid about £13 and four tons of coal a year. City Road, built in 1882, cut off the green lawn in front of the hospital and caused the resiting of the part nearer the hospital.

In the 18th and early 19th centuries the land to the north of the Holy Jesus was occupied by the Poor House, the Bridewell (House of Correction) and a Charity School, all of which have now disappeared but in 1880 the Police Station which adjoined the Holy Jesus on the west was replaced by a Soup Kitchen which was built to harmonize with its more substantial neighbour.

Shortly before the Second World War the hospital was declared unfit and a new Holy Jesus Hospital was built at Spital Tongues in 1937. N. Pevsner describes the hospital as a "building of honest character". It's style is unusual for Newcastle showing Italian and Dutch influence. Inside is a fine dark oak staircase whose carvings were removed to Spital Tongues in 1937.

At the back of the Holy Jesus Hospital is a 13th century tower remaining from the Austin Friary, probably a part of the gate which Bourne described in 1736.

Steam Soup

MANUFACTORY.

The Public are respectfully informed, that there is now ready for Sale, at the Manufactory in the Manors,

SOUP,

composed of One Pound of Beef to every Gallon, with Vegetables and proper Seasonings in Proportion, at the *low Price* of *One Penny a Pint*, or *Eight-pence a Gallon.*

SOUP, in the Process of Boiling, is not unfrequently burnt, and its Flavour injured; but when prepared by Steam, this is prevented, and great Part of the Liquid becomes pure distilled Water by the Condensation of the Steam. Thus the Soup is made peculiarly rich, pleasant, and wholesome, and forms a highly nutritious Food for Persons of all Ages.

*** The Soup will be ready for Sale between 8 and 12 o'Clock every working Day.

Newcastle upon Tyne.

Mackenzie and Dent, Printers.

Crossing the road in front of the Holy Jesus Hospital and following the walk-way towards the Tyne Bridge brings us to All Saint's Church.

The medieval church of **All Saints** was demolished and rebuilt by David Stephenson in 1786-96. It is architecturally a building of great interest with "many elements of genuine grace and beauty joined to others of clumsy deformity". It is on a splendid site and this round church with its striking spire is conspicuous to the visitor approaching from the south.

left: All Saints, formerly All Hallows

Newcastle with the spire of All Saints dominating the skyline. *G. Balmer, 1836*

From All Saints we can go by a complicated underpass to the bottom of Pilgrim Street to view what is known as Alderman Fenwick's House, though more recently it was the Liberal Club and before 1884 was the Queen's Head Inn.

Alderman Fenwick's House is a large rambling house and although altered considerably inside still retains a fine old staircase with fat turned balusters. It has a long stable yard extending as far as Grey Street. With its projecting wings standing on rusticated pillars and fine old brickwork it still presents a picturesque appearance.

It was probably built early in the 18th century but in the lounge "there is a plaster ceiling in the Jacobean tradition, which, if original, indicates a structure older than the façade". The building is illustrated on Corbridge's map of 1773 and described as Alderman Fenwick's house. In the days of the stage coach it was one of the chief coaching inns of the town.

Retracing our steps a little down Pilgrim Street and turning into Mosely Street we come to the junction of Dean Street and Grey Street. Dean Street was created in the last years of the 18th century. Although no buildings here are of outstanding merit the decorated facades of many are very attractive.

Grey Street *J.W. Carmichael, 1842*

Grey Street, which is admired by all visitors to our city, is the crowning work of Grainger and Dobson. In the eighteenth century the site was a valley with a stream running through it called the Lort Burn. Grainger had to fill this in before building his street. At the top of the valley once stood the Greyfriars' Monastery. After the Dissolution of the Monasteries Robert Anderson, a wealthy Newcastle merchant built a fine mansion called the Newe House on the site. In 1675 it came into the hands of the Blacketts from whom it was bought in 1783 by George Anderson a wealthy architect who re-named the house Anderson Place. In 1832 Grainger bought the house and gardens for £50,000 and demolished it to make room for Grey Street.

The chief ornament on the east side is the **Theatre Royal**, with its fine portico, designed by Benjamin Green. The interior however was gutted by a fire in 1899 and had to be entirely reconstructed in a different style. At the top end of the street is the triangular Central Arcade based on the Corinthian temple of Vesta at Tivoli. The building once housed an Art Gallery, News Room and a theatre called the Vaudeville. However the interior was destroyed by fire and the present Central Arcade within the walls of the Exchange Buildings was constructed in 1906.

At the junction of Grainger Street and Grey Street stands **Grey's Monument**, the monument to Earl Grey of Howick the prime minister responsible for the passing of the Reform Bill. It is an Ionic column 41.1m [135ft] in height surmounted by a statue by Bailey. An internal staircase of 164 steps takes one to the summit from which there is a fine panoramic view of the city.

Grey Street, looking towards Grey's Monument with the Theatre Royal on the right. *c. 1850*

From the middle of Grey Street a narrow lane called High Bridge leads to the Bigg Market. Along with the Cloth Market and the Groat Market these three streets are an historic area of Newcastle.

These streets have been considerably altered over the years but we can still picture them as they were 200 years ago. The **Bigg Market** derives its name from the sale of bigg, a particular kind of barley. Previously it was called the Oat Market. At one time there was a fine view of St Nicholas from the Bigg Market but it was obscured by the erection of the Town Hall, which has itself been replaced by a modern complex of buildings. The area has always been a centre of entertainment with countless pubs. A number have survived. Bewick's old pub, the **Black Boy** can still be visited.

Here met the famous Swarley's Club of which Bewick said in his 'Memoirs': "This was the most rational society or meeting I ever knew. The few rules which bound us together were only verbal. The first was that every member should conduct himself with decorum, and as a gentleman. If anyone transgressed on this point he was immediately fined, and if he did not pay, he was sent to Coventry, or dismissed. On entering the room, every member paid fourpence, which was to be spent in refreshment. There were no regular debatings allowed on any subject but such as might occasionally arise out of the passing conversation, and the company separated at ten o'clock. Such a place of meeting proved convenient and pleasant to many a stranger who visited the town, and the expense was as nothing."

Undoubtedly the most famous place in the Cloth Market is **Balmbra's**, Tyneside's Music Hall. Newcastle was one of the first cities to possess a Music Hall. In the 1850s Harmonic Meetings were held at the Royal Hotel and Music Saloon in Grainger Street. At the Scotch Arms in the Bigg Market sing-songs had long been held while the Tyne Concert Hall had been opened in 1838. But real Music Hall started when John Balmbra moved from the Royal Hotel to the Wheatsheaf in 1858. Four years later Geordie Ridley first sang the *Blaydon Races* here. In 1865 the 'singing room' was enlarged and called the Oxford Music Hall. For many years the Geordie Music Hall flourished at Balmbra's but towards the end of the century the competition of the Variety Theatre proved too strong. It closed down and changed into a Billiard Hall called the Carlton Hotel. However in 1962 the centenary of the Blaydon Races, it was reopened and for a while flourished as Britain's oldest surviving Music Hall. The famous Tyneside comedian, Dick Irwin, presided here for many years.

In a cul-de-sac is the **Old George** one of the oldest and most picturesque inns in Newcastle. Its history is very unclear but almost certainly it dates from the 17th century. That Charles I regularly visited the place when he was a prisoner of the Scots in Newcastle is pure legend. The Old George did however become an important coaching inn and was a favourite resort of the farmers who attended the nearby Corn Market.

Groat Market, 1850

From the Bigg Market we turn into Grainger Street.

The **Grainger Market**, in its time, was "considered the most spacious and magnificent in Europe". It was part of the Grainger Dobson development of central Newcastle and opended October 24th, 1835. Originally there were two sections, the Butcher and Green Markets, and today these two sections are still predominant.

Proceeding along Grainger Street we come to St John's Church.

St John's Church (built c.1287) with its well worn stone, small size and simplicity it reminds one of a country church. With its churchyard and fine trees, an oasis of green in central Newcastle, this resemblance is increased.

Overlooking St John's is the **Central Station**. It was opened in 1850 by Queen Victoria. With its two miles of platforms it is a magnificent creation of the Industrial Revolution. The architect was John Dobson although it was not completed entirely to his design. The platforms are curved and the roof is an outstanding example of 19th century iron work. The entrance has an impressive portico. Attached to the station is the Station Hotel with sumptuous decorated rooms of fine design the like of which will never be built again.

From the Station a short walk brings us to the **Library of the Literary and Philosophical Society** which stands at the beginning of Westgate Road. This neo-Grecian building was built by John Green from1822-5. The earliest debating Society in Newcastle was called 'The Philosophical Society' and was formed in 1775. The present 'Lit and Phil' was established in 1793.

Nearby at the bottom of Westgate Road stands a **monument to George Stephenson**. The great inventor stands on a pedestal; around the base are the figures of a miner, engineer, navvy and smith. The monument was erected in 1862 at a cost of £5,000. The sculptor was W. G. Lough.

A short walk up Westgate Road brings us to the **Assembly Rooms**. Built in 1776 the Assembly Rooms is one of the finest buildings in Newcastle and has played an important part in the social life of the city. However sixty years before, the old Assembly Rooms stood on the opposite side of the street where dances and masquerades were held until about 1736 when new rooms were built in the Groat Market. Here the wealthy people of Newcastle held their meetings for 40 years until the present building was erected.

The new Assembly Rooms cost £6,000. There were 129 share holders holding 234 shares of £25 each and the Corporation donated £200. William Newton's building, in the Adam style, was an ornament to the city. The Great Ball Room, with its fine plasterwork and magnificent chandeliers is the gem of the building. A brochure tells us that "the seven gorgeous chandeliers of scintillating crystal depending from the ceiling are superb in their brilliance". The centre chandelier, a massive gem, is reputed to have cost 600 guineas, and it is interesting to note that these chandeliers have now been used for three methods of lighting, by candle, gas and electricity.

Newcastle Town Walls

Although the walls of the borough are mentioned in a charter of King John dated 1216 it wasn't until the second half of the century, probably in the reign of Edward I, that the work was started. By that time the town had achieved self-government and had expanded commercially. When in 1334 Edward III stayed at the Blackfriars to receive homage from Edward Baliol for the kingdom of Scotland he repaired the walls of the town. In 1342 they proved their worth by keeping at bay King David of Scotland and a large army and in 1388 once more foiled a Scottish force.

When during the Civil War Newcastle was once again attacked the walls were sufficiently strong to hold at bay an army of 30,000 men for almost three months. But in the final assault the walls were so damaged that a later parliament granted £2,564 for repairing them. During the rebellion of 1745 the town was again put in a posture of defence, the walls were backed with earth and guns placed on them and even during the Napoleonic Wars they were considered of sufficient importance to be repaired and garrisoned. However their utility was now over and they were allowed to fall into decay and sections were demolished. Today what is left is being carefully restored and preserved.

The famed walls of Newcastle consisted of a strong curtain wall, with towers, turrets and gatehouses. The wall varied in thickness and height. Between the Morden and Heber towers they were 2.1m [7ft] thick and 6.1m [20ft] high to the parapet walk. Access to the walls was only possible at the towers and gatehouses. The parapet walk overhung the inner walls being supported on corbels.

The **turrets** were mainly intended as look-outs which gave protection in bad weather although there was a single loophole for an archer with a recess at the back to give him room to draw his bow. On the front the turret was flush with the curtain face but the back projected on corbels. There was an external staircase which gave access to the roof which was battlemented with machicolations to the front.

Most of the **towers** were of a similar pattern, rectangular on the inner side and semi-circle on the exterior. The rounded tower was much stronger than the early medieval rectangular tower it replaced since they had no blind spots and were less easily mined. The Heber Tower, the most perfect still standing, is typical. It is only one storey high with a stone vault to carry the roof. It has three large cross loopholes, one facing outwards and the other two covering the curtain walls on either side. The tower has large stone corbels which were intended to support wooden hoardings. These were erected only in time of war. They projected over the battlements and had windows to shoot through. The roof was reached by an external staircase.

All the main **gates** were fortified gate houses of great strength. The New Gate and the West Gate were the most important, the latter having a barbican in front. There were also a number of postern gates, salley ports, water gates giving access to the river and a gate on the Tyne Bridge. In 1280 the Black Friars were granted a postern gate to give access to their garden outside the wall. This still remains although it is now blocked with stone.

West Gate *T.M. Richardson, Senior* *Etching*

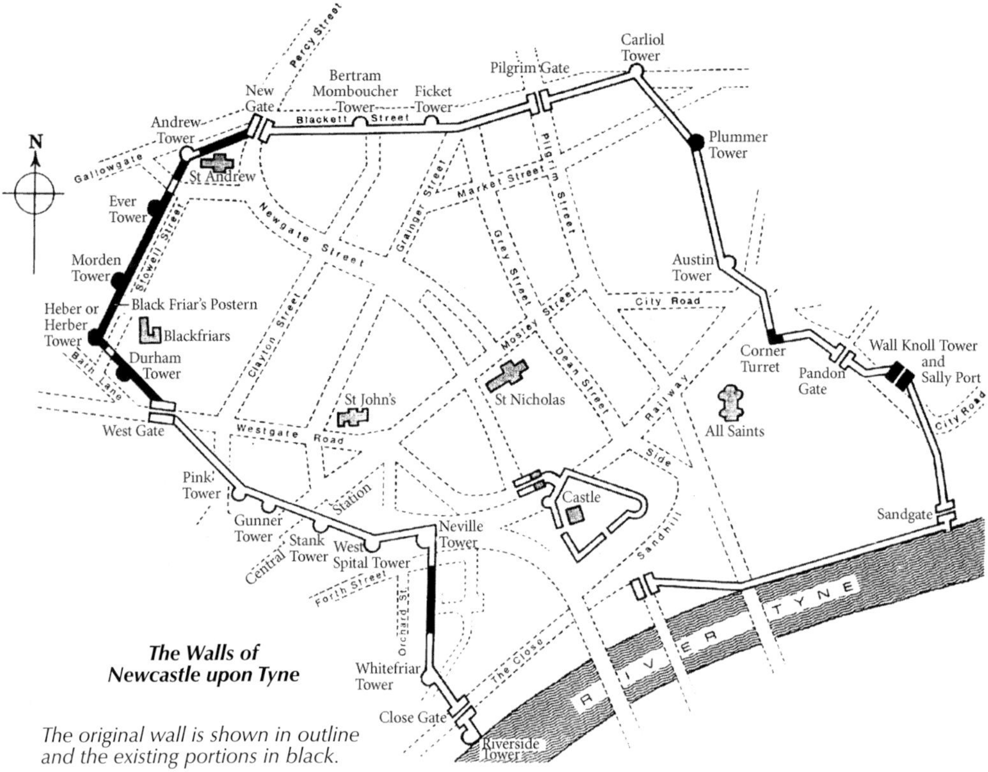

The Walls of Newcastle upon Tyne

The original wall is shown in outline and the existing portions in black.

The Walls Today

If we start on the east side the first portion of the wall clearly visible is the Wall Knoll Tower and **Sally-Port**. It is often called the Carpenters' Tower because the company of Carpenters or Shipwrights met in it. In the year 1716 they built above it "a grand and stately square tower adorned at the top corners with four fair turrets, built in the form of a lanthorn". The postern gate in this tower was used for sallying forth to attack the besiegers and from this circumstance has been called the Sally-Port Gate. It presents a picturesque but very unmilitary appearance today. The street in which it stands is called Tower Street.

On the south side of City Road near Manors Station can be seen the remains of **Corner Turret,** so called from being in an angle of the wall, and part of the wall.

Travelling north we come to **Plummer Tower** in Croft Street, a tower which has been considerably altered. It has gone under a variety of names such as Carliol Croft Tower and Cutler's Tower. In 1742 it was granted to the fraternity of Masons by whom it was repaired "and fronted in a handsome manner". A portion of the curtain wall and part of the original circular outer face can be seen among the rebuilding. All the northern wall has disappeared until we reach St Andrew's Church.

Near **St Andrew's churchyard** can be seen a stretch of the curtain wall. On the portion near Darn Crook can be seen the corbels which on the inside supported the walk along the walls.

Wall turret, St Andrew's churchyard. *S. Holmes, 1895*

We now come to **The West Walls**, a long stretch of wall in good condition with substantial remains of four towers. We can pass along the pomerium (or road behind the walls) now called Back Stowell Street and see the walls from the inside. We can also see along the front from Darn Crook, and from Bath Lane. There is little to be seen of the first tower, the Ever Tower. The other three the Durham, Heber and Morden Towers were originally similar in design and probably built at the same time, i.e. about 1280. Internally they are rectangular but rounded to the field. The Morden Tower has a storey added in 1620 when it belonged to the Company of Plumbers, Glaziers and Pewterers and was used as their meeting place. Further alterations were made in 1700. The Heber Tower is the most perfect remaining, on the walls of Newcastle. It was one storey high with a stone ribbed vault supporting the roof. The walls were pierced by three large cross loops. A stone stair leads to the roof which it embattled. The battlements are not original but were modified probably during the Civil War to take guns. At the junction of the wall with the tower is a projecting latrine, with a small loop-hole in the battlements above to protect it. The tower was occupied by the Feltmakers Company in 1620.

The turret between the Morden and Heber Towers is the best preserved on the wall. It shows the passage way and the outside staircase to the roof. The battlements of the wall have been built up in this section and the parapet heightened, work probably carried out at the time of the Napoleonic Wars. The Durham Tower is in a good state of preservation and the section of the wall here has been carefully restored. The wall crossed Westgate Road at the West Gate and from this point little of the wall has survived. The Gunner Tower has disappeared under Pink Lane and the Stank Tower was where the Central Station portico now stands.

Sally-Port Tower

In Orchard Street a section of the wall, preserved to its full height, can be seen and nearby another short length stands at the end of Hanover Square .

From here nothing remains of the wall although the site of the Close Gate is marked by a stone with the inscription *Site of the Town Wall*. It is on the north side of The Close east of the bonded warehouse. Everything along the river front has disappeared including the famous Sand Gate.

Close to the Tower Walls and near Stowell Street, stand the remains of **Blackfriars** monastery. The house was built some time before 1239 by Peter Scott, first mayor of Newcastle. Here in 1334 Edward Baliol, King of Scotland, did homage to Edward I. The monastery must have been well equipped since it was the usual place of residence when royalty visited Newcastle. Until recent times the surviving buildings were used by some of the town guilds. Over one of the doors we can see this inscription: *By hammer and hand, All artes do stand.*

Blackfriars' Monastery

Approximately a hundred metres from Blackfriars is the ancient church of St Andrew's tucked in behind the city walls and near the former Newgate.

St Andrew's Church is probably the oldest church in the town. Part of the tower is 12th century work and contains Roman stones. The church has seen many alterations and additions during its long history so that many styles of ecclesiastical architecture can be seen. It was badly damaged during the siege of 1644 when the Scottish cannon breached the town walls nearby. Internally the oldest portion is the Norman chancel arch, lofty and wide, richly decorated with zigzag ornamentation. The nave arcades are probably of the same date. In the church is the tomb of William Newton architect of St Ann's church and the old Assembly Rooms, who died in 1797.

above: St Andrew's by T.M. Richardson, 1902

opposite: Our illustration, by John Knox from McKenzie's History of Newcastle *(1827), is an artist's impression executed when Eldon Square was still being built – the original design seems to have been modified.*

Haymarket

From St Andrew's we proceed up Percy Street passing the huge Eldon Square complex to the Haymarket a name recalling Newcastle's role as a market for agricultural produce. On one side of the square we find part of Newcastle University. **The Museum of Antiquities** here houses a magnificent collection of Roman remains. Opposite is the church of **St Thomas** built by John Dobson 1825-30 and behind that the **Civic Centre**.

North of the Haymarket, overlooking the motorway is the **Hancock Museum**. It looks as though it was built by Dobson but actually the architect was John Wardle and the date is 1878-1885. It is named after Albany Hancock (1806-73) and John Hancock (1808-90) famous Newcastle naturalists.

Eldon Square, one of the finest works of Richard Grainger, was designed by John Dobson and Thomas Oliver. The houses were built to a uniform design of exceptional quality with spacious gardens in front. When completed in 1831 they attracted considerable attention. Such superior houses had never been seen in the North. Most have now been demolished to make way for the Eldon Square Shopping Centre.

The **Civic Centre** was opened in 1968. Many buildings arose in Newcastle during the second half of the 20th century but almost alone the Civic Centre had few critics. It was designed by the City architect George Kenyon. The Council Chamber is elliptical in shape and is the focal point of the façade to the Great North Road. The tower behind is crowned with a lantern and beacon and contains a carillon of 25 bells which, on occasions, play a selection of local tunes. The tower is clearly inspired by the tower of St Nicholas Cathedral. The interior is lavishly decorated and designed. Outstanding parts of the building are the Great Stair Hall, the Banqueting Hall and the Lord Mayor's and Sheriff's suites whose gallery contains the city Regalia and treasures.

Originally the **Town Moor**, the Castle Leazes and the Forth were the common pastures of the town. In 1647 grassmen were appointed to look after the pastures on the Moor. About 1650 the Nun's Moor which originally belonged to the Nuns of St Bartholomew was bought by the Corporation and added to the Town Moor. In 1771 there was a dispute between the freemen and the town magistrates about the ownership of the Moor and the Town Council won. The ownership of the Moor was vested in the Corporation but the rights of herbage were granted to the freemen who were each entitled to pasture two milch cows there.

The Town Moor has been used for many purposes. In the 13th century coal was mined here. It was a favourite spot for public executions, Gallowgate reminds us today of the route taken from the prison to the place of execution. In 1829 a woman was taken for hanging in a cart "sitting above her coffin" with a crowd of 20,000 to witness the event. The last public execution on the Moor was in 1844. Cricket was played here from 1827. A bull was baited here in 1774 by the freemen. Two annual fairs were held on the Moor. Cow Hill Fair was one of the largest horse and cattle fairs in the country.

VIEW
OF
The Grand Stand, &c.
NEWCASTLE.

Horse racing started on the Town Moor in 1721, being transferred from Killingworth Moor; and a Grandstand was erected in 1800. In 1882 the races were transferred to Gosforth and a Temperance Festival took their place on the Moor. Out of this grew the famous 'Hoppings' which we know today. The Newcastle United Golf Club whose members play on the Moor was founded in 1891. The Town Moor was also a favourite rendezvous for political meetings. The miners, the Chartists and Reformers at various times have assembled on the Moor in meetings of record numbers.